D1521974

BIDEN
UNPLUGGED

EVERY UNSCRIPTED, COHERENT, AND POLITICALLY CORRECT MOMENT WITH JOE BIDEN

VERA FUHNAY
POLITICAL ANALYST

ISBN: 9798686654471

Back cover photo:
Lienemann, D., photographer. (2013) Official portrait of Vice President Joe Biden in his West Wing office at the White House / Official White House photo by David Lienemann. , 2013. [Photograph] Retrieved from the Library of Congress, https://www.loc.gov/item/2017645542/.

A gift for you

Enjoy your gift! From Marja Thompson

amazon Gift Receipt

Send a Thank You Note

You can learn more about your gift or start a return here too.

Scan using the Amazon app or visit
https://a.co/fdB6uka

Biden Unplugged: A Blank Book Novelty Gag Gift With Every Unscripted, Coherent, and Politically Correct Moment With Joe ...

Order ID: 114-5452829-1109045   Ordered on June 24, 2021

Made in the USA
Middletown, DE
16 June 2021